John St Nicholas died aged 94 in 1698. He was a Puritan who thus lived through the turmoil of the seventeenth century. The particular interest of this lecture lies in his ministry in 'retirement' following his ejection from Lutterworth at the Restoration. Here we see the opportunities as well as the perils of such a ministry.

Revd Mark Burkill, Chair of Latimer Trust

For all my 'friends in Leicestershire'

St Antholin's Lecture 2022

From Barebones to Old Bones

John St Nicholas (1604–1698): Godly Usefulness in Later Life

Lesley A. Rowe

The Latimer Trust

The Latimer Trust (formerly Latimer House, Oxford) is a conservative Evangelical research organisation within the Church of England, whose main aim is to promote the history and theology of Anglicanism as understood by those in the Reformed tradition. Interested readers are welcome to consult its website for further details of its many activities.

The Latimer Trust
London N14 4PS UK
Registered Charity: 1084337
Company Number: 4104465
Web: www.latimertrust.org
E-mail: administrator@latimertrust.org

CONTENTS

Introduction

Recently I reached a significant milestone; I became eligible to receive the State Pension. I am officially old. As such, I am part of an ageing demographic: according to the Office for National Statistics, there are currently 12.2 million people over sixty-five in the UK, and that figure is expected to rise to 16.5 million by 2036.[1] How should we all approach our later years, and what can Christians of previous generations teach us on this subject?

For almost thirty years, the hours of my life have been marked by the chiming of St Catherine's church clock close to my house in the Leicestershire village of Burbage. As I began research for a series of lectures on the Great Ejection of 1662, I was amazed to discover that one of the thirty-five Leicestershire Bartholomeans was buried only a stone's throw away, in the chancel of St Catherine's in his ninety-fifth year.[2] John St Nicholas (pronounced '*Seniclas*') had been ejected from his living after the Restoration of the monarchy, but subsequently lived on for a further thirty-eight years. This booklet, very much an exercise in 'practical divinity', will focus on how John St Nicholas used his time during his lengthy 'retirement', which I hope will serve as a helpful model for Christians today seeking to continue serving God into old age.

---

[1] '"Thousands" of retirement villages needed', *The Times*, 10 October 2022, 44.

[2] Those ministers ejected because they could not subscribe to the Act of Uniformity, which came into force on 24 August 1662 (St Bartholomew's Day in the church calendar), were commonly referred to as Bartholomeans.

It will initially touch on the seventeenth-century historical background, to set St Nicholas in context, briefly trace the course of his life up to the time of the Ejection, and then concentrate in rather more detail on his life thereafter.

The seventeenth-century historical background

John St Nicholas's life spanned almost the whole of the turbulent seventeenth century. Politically and religiously, it was a time of great upheaval and change. John Coffey offers this snapshot of the ecclesiastical situation in 1600, only four years before St Nicholas's birth:

> England had no permanent settlements in America, and little Protestant dissent from the Established Church. By 1600, the internal Presbyterian challenge to the episcopal polity of the Church of England appeared to have been foiled. Separatists had been brutally supressed in the 1590s, and while some breakaway congregations persisted in London, East Anglia and the Midlands, they were tiny, scattered, and exceedingly vulnerable. As yet there were no Congregational 'gathered churches', no English Baptists and no Quakers. With the exception of a few thousand Separatists and perhaps 40,000 Catholic recusants, the English (and Welsh) worshipped in the 9,000 or so parishes of the national church ... Richard Hooker

could write that there was not 'any man
of the commonwealth, which is not also
of the Church of England'.[3]

A century later, two years after St Nicholas's death, the
picture looked dramatically different. Coffey continues:
'The Dissenters boasted around 2000 congregations in
England and Wales, many with hundreds of members
... England had become a religiously fragmented society
divided between different denominations and between
"Church" and "Dissent".'

The story of how that change came about is one that is
probably familiar to most of us, at least in outline: the rise
in religious tensions caused by the policies of Archbishop
Laud and the Stuart monarchs; the Great Migration of
about 30,000 nonconformists to New England to escape
persecution in the 1630s; the Civil Wars, the execution
of King Charles I, and the years of religious liberty and
debate during the Commonwealth and Protectorate
periods under Oliver Cromwell in the 1640s and 1650s.
The death of Cromwell and the inadequacy of his son
Richard saw the collapse of the godly experiment to
reform the Church of England. The initial hopes of
religious toleration at the Restoration of Charles II in
1660 soon evaporated. The bishops and their allies in
the 'Cavalier' Parliament were implacable, embarking,
in David Appleby's words, 'upon a quest to secure
church and state by implementing a rigid and exclusive

---

[3] John Coffey, 'Introduction', in *The Oxford History of Protestant Dissenting Traditions*, vol. 1 (Oxford: Oxford University Press, 2020):1–2.

Anglican orthodoxy in local government and the parish pulpit'.[4] The punitive enactments of the Clarendon Code officially pushed those with nonconformist consciences outside the Church of England. And still to come before the century ended was persecution, plague, the Fire of London, and the Glorious Revolution.

John St Nicholas was not only an onlooker during all of these events, he also played a part in the narrative and his life was shaped by the experiences.

Biography of John St Nicholas pre-ejection

John was born in 1604 into an ancient gentry family in Ash, near Sandwich in Kent.[5] Socially and religiously, the family was part of that group which was to form the backbone of parliamentary support as the century progressed. His father, Thomas, was a pious, scholarly man with an excellent library – Tremellius's Latin Bible in folio was his prize possession. In 1619, aged fifteen, John matriculated as a student at Emmanuel College, Cambridge during the latter years that Laurence Chaderton was Master. His elder brother Thomas,

[4] David J. Appleby, *Black Bartholomew's Day: Preaching, Polemic and Restoration Nonconformity* (Manchester: Manchester University Press, 2007), 2.

[5] I am indebted to H. Neville Davies, ed., *At Vacant Hours: Poems by Thomas St Nicholas and his Family* (Birmingham: University of Birmingham, 2002) for much of this biographical information. Details are also taken from John Nichols, *The History and Antiquities of Leicestershire*, vol. IV, part I (1807):269–71, and part II (1811):464–65; A. G. Matthews, *Calamy Revised* (Oxford: Clarendon, 1934), and Samuel Palmer, *The Nonconformist's Memorial* (1775).

eighteen months his senior, matriculated at the same time. The St Nicholas brothers shared chambers and remained close all their lives, having lost their mother when they were very young boys. They were united in their love for the Reformed faith and in their parliamentary sympathies. After Cambridge, their ways parted, Thomas entering the Inns of Court, and John living with family near Ely for a while.

John's godly convictions were manifested in his financial backing of the early nonconformist colonists who had settled in Massachusetts from 1629. Although John St Nicholas did not actually emigrate himself, he continued to take an interest in events there; he later dedicated a book to the governors and ministers of New England, declaring himself to be, 'a sympathiser in your joys, fears and sorrows, a spectator and observer of the mutual transactings twixt God and you'.[6]

By 1630, John had married Etheldreda Goode of Stretton-under-Fosse near Rugby in Warwickshire, and they went on to have four children who survived infancy. John and his family retained close links with that area, and between 1653 and 1656 he was to be found officiating at several marriages in Monks Kirby parish church which served the village of Stretton.[7] However, by the early

---

[6] John St Nicholas, *The History of Baptism* (London, 1678), Frontispiece.

[7] Nichols, *History of Leicestershire*, IV.I:271. Extracts from the parish register of Monks Kirby were communicated to Nichols by the then current vicar Rev. R. P. Podmore. These showed 'Under the Usurpation, 1653, 4, 5, and 6, there are several Marriages "before me, John St Nicholas"'.

1650s John and his wife were living in Lutterworth, just across Watling Street (now the A5) in Leicestershire, where he was probably acting in the capacity of lecturer at St Mary's church, in place of the sequestered rector.[8] John was nominated to the living by the parliamentary sequestrators and officially appointed as rector of Lutterworth in early 1659.[9] It must have been a great honour for him to minister in the renowned John Wycliffe's church in Lutterworth, the place where the English Bible originated. The presumption is that John St Nicholas must have received presbyterian ordination at some stage.

But the 1650s were a sad time, too, for John: two of his children, his daughter Abigail and his eighteen-year-old son Vincent, a London apprentice, were buried

[8] The residence of the family in Lutterworth, says Nichols, *History of Leicestershire*, IV.I:270, is obliquely marked by the entry in the registers of the name of Mr Timothy St Nicholas (John's son) as a witness to a marriage in February 1654, and of John himself as a witness to three marriages in 1654 and 1656. The burials of John's wife and children in Lutterworth in 1653 and 1654 also attest to the fact. Nathaniel Tovey was rector of Lutterworth in 1630 but had been sequestered by 1646, for various offences including absenteeism, neglecting to use the Directory of Worship, and refusal to give the sacrament except at the altar rails. An interim rector, John Moore, was appointed in July 1647, but being 'forcibly kept out' remained at Clavering, Essex, from where he himself was ejected due to sequestration in 1662 (see A. G. Matthews, *Walker Revised* (Oxford: Clarendon, 1948), 246–47 and *Calamy Revised*, 352). It was during the confusion and turmoil of these years in the early 1650s, that St Nicholas began his ministry in Lutterworth.
[9] Composition of first-fruits, a sum payable on admission to a new living, was paid by St Nicholas for Lutterworth in March 1659, see Matthews, *Calamy Revised*, 423.

in Lutterworth church in 1653, followed by his wife
Etheldreda in 1654. Overshadowed by this personal
loss, in 1653, John was nominated on the approval of
Oliver Cromwell to the short-lived Barebones Parliament
(sometimes called 'The Parliament of the Saints'),
representing Warwickshire.[10] His brother Thomas, now
a parliamentary army administrator, was nominated for
Yorkshire. Thomas St Nicholas served on the Council
of State, but John's contribution seems to have been
less prominent. However, he was appointed to serve on
the committee for the advancement of learning in July
1653 and was named as a commissioner for his county
in the ordinance of 1654 for the ejecting of scandalous,
ignorant, disaffected, and otherwise unworthy ministers.[11]
In 1658 and 1659 John signed the Leicestershire
Addresses expressing loyalty to Richard Cromwell and
the parliament.

In 1657, aged fifty-three, John St Nicholas married for the
second time, travelling the nine miles or so up Watling
Street from Lutterworth to Burbage. His new wife was
forty-two-year-old Lady Priscilla Grey, youngest daughter

---

[10] See the History of Parliament website for more details of the nominated
Assembly, which had about 140 members and was dissolved in December
1653. Parliamentary historian Dr Vivienne Larminie provides a more
nuanced assessment of the much-derided Assembly, its membership
and activity.

[11] 'Guibon Goddard's Journal: July 1653', in *Diary of Thomas Burton
Esq: July 1653–April 1657*, ed. John Towill Rutt (London, 1828), i–iv.
British History Online http://www.british.history.ac.uk/burton-diaries/vol
1/i.iv (accessed 17 August 2022); Austin Woolrych, *Commonwealth to
Protectorate* (Oxford: Oxford University Press, 1982), 427.

of Anthony Grey, the former rector of St Catherine's, Burbage. Anthony Grey (who had died twelve years previously) was a remarkable man and greatly beloved. He was a resolute puritan who had ministered in Burbage for fifty years when he unexpectedly inherited the title of ninth Earl of Kent when he was aged eighty-two. Many pressed him to quit the ministry but he 'did not in the least abate the constancy of his preaching, so long as he was able to be led up into the pulpit'.[12] The only difference his new title seemed to make was that he was no longer molested by the authorities for his nonconformity, as he had been when he was plain Mr Anthony Grey. Priscilla Grey remained in Burbage after her father's death to care for her widowed mother Magdalen, who died in 1653.

John and Priscilla did not live in Lutterworth very long after their marriage, since John was ejected in 1660, to make way for the very elderly and ailing royalist Thomas Pestell. Pestell appears to have neglected his new charge and lived in Leicester.[13]

Although St Nicholas was ejected before 1662, his views meant that in conscience he would not have been able to conform to any of the clauses in the Act of Uniformity. We know that he was a faithful supporter of the parliamentary cause (though opposed to the regicide). As someone

---

[12] Nichols, *History of Leicestershire*, IV.II:458. Nichols also includes a quote from the *Magna Britannia* about Grey: 'He was no more affected with the addition of titles, than a corpse with a fine coffin; and made no other use of his honours, than to support goodness, and make his doctrine more effectual'.

[13] See Davies, *At Vacant Hours*, 319.

with presbyterian views, he is likely to have signed the Solemn League and Covenant, which he would have been required to renounce. If he had been ordained by a presbyterian classis he may have objected to the demand for reordination by a bishop.[14] Almost certainly he would have taken issue, too, with some things in the new Prayer Book. However, in common with the majority of those labelled as presbyterians he believed in the idea of a national church (though more thoroughly reformed), and desired comprehension rather than separation. Like Richard Baxter, he may have preferred to be known as a 'meer Christian'.[15]

Post-Ejection: John St Nicholas's retirement years

On ejection, John and his wife retired to live in Burbage, where Priscilla had inherited 'considerable property'.[16] Of the several possible locations, it appears most likely that their place of residence was the Manor House, or White House, near the centre of the village.[17] Priscilla

---

[14] During the Interregnum (from c. 1646–1659), the Church of England was officially governed according to a presbyterian rather than an episcopal system. Ordination and matters of church discipline were to be carried out by local groups of ministers and lay elders assembled in a 'classis' or presbytery, rather than by a bishop as was formerly the case. In practice, the establishment of classes was patchy.

[15] For a more nuanced discussion of Baxter's taxonomy of parties, see Lee Gatiss, 'The Autobiography of a "Meer Christian"', *Churchman* 122/2 (2008):159–75.

[16] Nichols, *History of Leicestershire*, IV.II:460.

[17] I would like to acknowledge the help given to me by local historians associated with the Burbage Heritage Group in attempting to ascertain where John lived in the village, and in searching for St Nicholas family

died in 1665, but John continued to live in Burbage until his death over thirty years later. He was a man of status and private means, with various properties in Leicestershire and Warwickshire and, unlike some other ejected ministers who were in dire financial straits, was not forced to make a living. But what was he to do next? Although the list is by no means comprehensive, there is evidence for the following activities:

1. Taking stock

The abrupt end to John St Nicholas's parish ministry must have caused him to take stock of his life, looking back over past years and contemplating how to approach the future. The puritans in general were famed for the practice of spiritual self-examination, and the auditing of their lives in the light of eternity. No one knew, of course, how long their allotted span would be, but death was a certainty for all. The 2021 St Antholin lecture focused on the keeping of journals as part of this exercise: John's brother Thomas kept a notebook of poems for the purpose.[18] Thomas, whose career of public service had also been terminated suddenly at the Restoration, conducted just such a spiritual audit of his own life in 1663, not long after he had reached the age of sixty. In a long and moving poem, Thomas meditated on the

graves in St Catherine's church and churchyard. In particular, Jo Garner-Williams for generously sharing draft pages of her forthcoming history of Burbage with me.

[18] Published as Kirsten Birkett, *Spiritual Practices of the Puritans: The Importance of Diary-keeping* (London: Latimer Trust, 2022).

The puritans in
general were famed
for the practice
of spiritual self-
examination, and the
auditing of their lives
in the light of eternity.

'arithmetic of Moses' in Psalm 90:12 ['So teach us, O Lord, to number our days, that we may apply our hearts to wisdom'], reviewing his past life at what he calls the 'fag-end of my pilgrimage', and desiring to know what work God would have him do in the days that lay ahead.[19] For Thomas that future was not a long one – he had a mere five years left.

Thomas's poem was probably written around the same date as a sermon in a manuscript notebook believed to be by John that includes the same exhortation, 'let us so number our days as to apply our hearts to true wisdom'.[20] Similar sentiments are expressed in other sermons preached in 1663, again attributed to John. At the funeral of a Mr Burbery on 19 March 1663, the preacher took as his text Job 16:22 ['When a few years are come, then I shall go the way whence I shall not return'].[21] He urges his hearers to contemplate their mortality and the inexorability of the grave. Unconverted listeners

---

[19] Thomas St Nicholas, 'The Recreation of an Accountant', in Davies, *At Vacant Hours*, 48–61.

[20] I owe a debt of gratitude to Davies, *At Vacant Hours*, 318, for alerting me to the existence of this manuscript volume of sermons preached in 1662–63, and now preserved in the Newberry Library, Chicago (N MS, Case MS C 991.767). This sermon dated 22 January 1663, (N MS, fol. 43r) is cited by Davies, *At Vacant Hours*, 280.

[21] I am very grateful to Dr Suzanne Karr Schmidt, George Amos Poole III Curator of Rare Books and Manuscripts at the Newberry Library, for photographing some of the manuscript sermon pages for me. This extract is from a sermon dated 19 March 1663 (N MS, fol. 70r), spelling and punctuation modernised.

are entreated to seek God while there is time, whereas believers are advised to:

> lay out all your strength for God; while you have opportunity do good, saith the apostle. Look upon yourself and think – this is the time I have allotted to improve my talent to the advantage of my master; this is the Lord's time and proportionable to my sowing here shall my reaping in glory be. Look upon your neighbours and friends and families and say, can death praise thee or they that go down to the grave with all thy wondrous works? No, if these receive any good by me it must be now; wherein I am able to stead [serve, help] them must be in this life; if I do not now exhort and instruct and teach and guide my family and those I am entrusted with, I shall never return from the grave to do it.

These injunctions are further underlined by an incident that happened in May 1663. Thomas St Nicholas and his wife Susanna had been travelling by coach from Kent to Burbage to pay John and Priscilla a visit, when, about twenty miles from their destination, the coach was overturned by a flash flood at Weedon, Northamptonshire. All would have perished but for a thorn bush preventing the coach sinking into the waters. Safely back home again in Kent after the visit, Thomas composed a long hymn of praise, giving thanks to God for his miraculous intervention. He sent a copy of this poem to John. John, a less accomplished poet, chose to reply in the same fashion to convey the joyful gratitude of 'your friends in Leicestershire' for God's mercy in sparing Thomas's life. John believed that it was vital to learn the lessons that God was trying to teach them through this providential deliverance, notably that the reason that they had been given more time on earth was in order to do some more good for God. John wrote:

> Lord, let thy warnings mind us what is past
> To keep us humble. Let the pleasant taste
> Of mercies in deliverance engage
> To serve thine honour with renewed courage,
> That, as thou giv'st us newly life to see,
> So may we give a life that's new to thee.
> Our soul from death now saved, our eyes from tears,
> Our feet from falling into dang'rous fears,
> To know thy righteous paths let our souls muse,
> Our eyes discern them; and our feet let use
> To walk this life as in thy presence, who,

'To know thy righteous paths let our souls muse,

Our eyes discern them; and our feet let use

To walk this life as in thy presence, who,

Hast made this life a land some good to do.'

Hast made this life a land some good
to do.[22]

Doing some good for God was thus the guiding principle
of John St Nicholas's remaining years, underpinning all
of his actions.

2. Fostering close relationships

This episode in 1663 also highlights the importance of
close relationships, never more necessary to John than
in retirement years. While his brother Thomas was alive,
they corresponded regularly, and, living some distance
from each other, obviously took pains to arrange visits.
In this way, the mutual encouragement and affection so
essential to both brothers was sustained. John had to cope
with a long period of widowhood (more than thirty years,
in his case) but he was fortunate to have the support of a
large extended family and network of friends who lived
locally, including his son Timothy and daughter Mercy.

In his poem, John mentions 'friends in Leicestershire'
and these may very well have included a group of fellow-
Bartholomeans who sought refuge in the nearby village
of Stoke Golding in the 1660s. Senior amongst these was
Nathaniel Stephens, former rector of Fenny Drayton. Of a
similar age to John, Stephens had been forced to contend
with the emergence of Quakerism in his parish, in the
form of George Fox. Stephens was not as long-lived as

---

[22] John St Nicholas, 'An Echo to 'An Hymn of Praise'; And for the
Deliverance, May 6, 1663', in Davies, *At Vacant Hours*, 73–75, quoted lines
93–104.

John, but he was remembered as being 'pleasant and cheerful' in his latter years. A friend recounted paying a visit to Stephens's home in Stoke Golding one day, when only Nathaniel and his wife Joan were at home. No one came to open the door in response to his knock but Nathaniel's voice called them to come in, asking 'whether of the two they would have had open the door for them, the blind or the lame? His wife being blind, and he so lame as not to be able to rise out of his chair without help'.[23]

3. Maintaining a farm

Retired people today often spend time on an allotment, enjoying the exercise, fresh air and a sense of gratification derived from growing their own produce. The inventory of John's property in Burbage, taken a month after his death in 1698, shows that he maintained a farm or substantial smallholding adjacent to his house. The livestock included a hog and two pigs, fifteen sheep, seven cows plus three yearling heifers with three calves, in addition to various crops in the fields and barn.[24] A significant number of ejected ministers were driven by necessity to take up farming to support their families, doing much of the hard agricultural work themselves. Although it seems unlikely that John would have undertaken much, if any, of the physical labour required in husbandry, he

---

[23] Palmer, *Nonconformist's Memorial*, 113.
[24] The Record Office for Leicestershire, Leicester and Rutland [ROLLR], Inventory of John St Nicholas, PR/1/103, 48/1698. Animals and crops alone are valued at over £40.

would still have had oversight of the enterprise.[25] Being able to supplement his income, provide fresh food for his own household, and to show hospitality to others at his table, must have brought him considerable satisfaction.

4. Continuing his calling

The ejected ministers referred to St Bartholomew's Day 1662, when the Act of Uniformity came into force, as the day of their 'civil death'. Their calling was to preach the gospel of Christ and to pastor their flocks, and now those who could not in conscience subscribe to the Act were legally barred from their parish pulpits. Supervening measures of the Clarendon Code restricted their preaching activities still further. Opinions differed as to what extent these ministers should obey the law, or defy it and suffer the penalties. John St Nicholas, like many others, still regarded himself as part of the Church of England and hoped for re-inclusion. He continued to attend parish services in St Catherine's for as long as he was physically able, as well as preaching to gatherings or conventicles which met at times that did not coincide with those services. If indeed the manuscript volume of sermons dated 1662–3 is the work of John St Nicholas, the sermons are likely to have been preached in or near

---

[25] Examples of ejected ministers labouring on their own farms include Thomas Wait, ex-vicar of Wetwang, East Yorkshire, and James King, former vicar of Debenham, Suffolk. For details see Matthews, *Calamy Revised*, 505, 309. King, it was reported, was forced to take a farm in order to subsist, 'And he used to sweat in Harvest, and endure the cold in Winter, that he might keep the lean wolf from the door'.

Being able to show
hospitality to others
at his table must
have brought him
considerable satisfaction.

Burbage in these years.[26] Under the Indulgence of 1672 John was licensed to preach as a 'Presbyterian' at his Burbage home, and in 1690 (when he was eighty-six) he is again reported as preaching in Burbage. In that same year of 1690 there is also mention of him preaching to a large congregation in nearby Hinckley, taking the place of his deceased son-in-law Henry Watts, another ejected minister whose third wife was St Nicholas's daughter Mercy.

John was only fifty-eight years old in 1662, and presumably still in his prime as a preacher. However, a note of caution needs to be raised at this point. It is very possible for a preacher to outstay his usefulness in pulpit terms: although John may have had excellent homiletical gifts aged fifty-eight, we do not know what he would have been like at eighty-six. The stamina and faithfulness of elderly preachers is something to be admired, but is it possible that the attempts to persuade his esteemed father-in-law Anthony Grey to stop preaching in his final years had as much to do with him being over eighty as to his becoming the Earl of Kent? Sometimes people are just too embarrassed or loyal to say anything. This was certainly the case with another ejected minister, Stephen Ford, former vicar of Chipping Norton, Oxfordshire, who went on to establish a Congregational church in Miles Lane, London. Twenty years later, when Ford was becoming decrepit, the church invited Matthew Clarke

---

[26] N MS, Case MS C 991.767, Newberry Library, Chicago, cited in Davies, *At Vacant Hours*, 319.

the younger from Market Harborough, Leicestershire, to minister alongside Ford. But it is recorded,

> It was sometime before the providence of God smiled upon this undertaking, for though the reverend Mr Ford was in the decline of life, he was unwilling to be thought to have outlived his usefulness, and therefore filled the pulpit oftener than was desired; this hindered the increase of the auditory, and together with some other unkindnesses which Mr Clarke met with, laid him under great discouragements.

When Clarke finally took over the whole of the work after the aged Ford's death in 1694, it is reported that 'within a year or two his auditory was crowded; vast additions were made to the church'.[27]

5. Showing practical kindness to other ejected ministers

John St Nicholas used his property and assets to help other ejected ministers in need.[28] John had a house at Knowle in Warwickshire and when he heard that James Wright, ejected from Wootton Wawen in the same county, had nowhere to go when displaced by the Five Mile Act in 1666, he wrote Wright a letter in which he 'invited

---

[27] Daniel Neal, *Sermons upon Several Occasions; By the Reverend Mr Matthew Clarke ... to which are added Some Memoirs of his Life, and the Sermon preach'd at his Funeral* (1727), xvi, xxiii–iv.
[28] See Matthews, *Calamy Revised*, 548.

him to Knoll, telling him there was a chamber, bed and study there, which he should be welcome to'. James Wright gratefully accepted the invitation, later keeping a school and preaching at the house. Another ejected minister who had fallen on hard times, old John Gilpin of Brinklow, was also able to live in the same house until his death soon after.[29] In addition, St Nicholas left 20 shillings in his will for the support of Richard Southwell, an ejected minister who had moved to Dadlington and was preaching at 'the meeting' in Hinckley.[30]

6. Keeping intellectually and spiritually active

In his later years, John continued to study the Scriptures and write books. It was said of him that he was 'an able scholar', 'who to the last', into his nineties, 'was used to style himself, a Student in St Paul's Epistles'.[31] This reveals both his humility and his desire to be always learning from God's word. In 1642, at the request of parliament, John had produced an English translation of a famous puritan work written in Latin, *The Marrow of Sacred Divinity* by William Ames, and in 1663 he issued *An Help to Beginners in the Faith* (apparently no longer

---

[29] Matthews, *Calamy Revised*, 223. See also Davies, *At Vacant Hours*, 199. The half-timbered building that became Blue Lake Cottages on Knowle Wood Rd has subsequently been demolished, but a drawing by Evelyn Wootton shows how they looked in the 1950s.

[30] Will of John St Nicholas, ROLLR, PR/1/103, 47 /1698. The 'Great Meeting' in Hinckley was established as a Presbyterian church but lapsed into Unitarianism in the eighteenth century.

[31] This quote, cited by Davies, *At Vacant Hours*, 320, is attributed to Edmund Calamy.

extant), which contained explanations of the Creed and the Lord's Prayer. This was followed by *The History of Baptism* in 1678, dedicated to the memory of his deceased father-in-law, Anthony Grey, and written with the purpose of encouraging unity between Christians.[32] John offered this work as 'the fruits of his retired thoughts in old age', asking allowance to be made for 'human infirmities'. He was surely thinking of Psalm 92:12–14 where the righteous are described as flourishing and still bearing fruit in old age – 'they are ever full of sap and green.'

Finally, in 1695, when he was ninety years old, John wrote what has been described as 'the final fruits of his attenuated old age', a pamphlet poignantly entitled *The Widow's Mite*, giving his exposition of Christ's sufferings, based on Luke 24:26.[33] Although it is beyond the scope of this booklet, both of these latter works, while showing a commendable desire for church unity, also display evidence of that Baxterian soteriology so ably critiqued by Dr James Packer in Volume Five of his *Puritan Papers*.[34]

7. Setting an example of steadfast faithfulness

Even as his capabilities declined with advanced age, John continued to live in Burbage in the 'Mansion House' and

---

[32] St Nicholas was writing from a paedobaptist perspective.

[33] Davies, *At Vacant Hours*, 320.

[34] J. I. Packer, 'The Doctrine of Justification Among the Puritans', from *Puritan Papers Vol. 5: 1968–69* (Phillipsburg, NJ: P&R Publishing, 2005). Packer writes that 'Baxter was a great and saintly man; as pastor, evangelist, and devotional writer, no praise for him can be too high; but as a theologian he was, though brilliant, something of a disaster'. I am grateful to Dr Samuel

set an example to others. As a man of high standing in local society, people took note of what he said and did. What was said of Rowland Nevet, a Shropshire Bartholomean, could equally have applied to John: 'When he could not do what he would, he did what he could'.[35] It is recorded that St Nicholas,

> went to the Public Church as long as he was able to go abroad, notwithstanding that he was for many years so thick of hearing, that he could not hear a word that was said. And when he was asked, why he would go to church when he had lost his hearing, he declared he went to give an Example to others, being afraid that if he should stay at home on the Lord's Day when there was a sermon in the church, others might be encouraged to stay at home, and keep from church too, though they had no such difficulty as he laboured under.[36]

Tunnicliffe for pointing me in the direction of this excellent article, and for discussions on post-Restoration theological and intellectual matters.

[35] Diary of Philip Henry, cited in Matthew Henry, *The Lives of Philip and Matthew Henry*, ed. J. B. Williams (Edinburgh: Banner of Truth, 1974), 271.

[36] Edmund Calamy, *An Account of the Ministers, Lecturers, Masters and Fellows of Colleges and Schoolmasters, who were Ejected or Silenced after the Restoration in 1660*, vol. II (1713):426. The comments are also recorded with slightly different wording in Nichols, *History of Leicestershire*, IV.I:270–71, and Matthews, *Calamy Revised*, 424.

'When he could not do
what he would, he did
what he could'.

When John first moved to Burbage, the rector of St Catherine's was John Pitts, a godly conformist, and Pitts and St Nicholas evidently shared a mutual respect. Pitts died in 1672, but John appears also to have had cordial relations with the two succeeding incumbents, James Duport and Robert Cotes.

Conclusion

In John St Nicholas's final years, deaf, and perhaps unable even to take the short walk from his house to the church, he lived, it is said, 'secluded from the world ... his principal amusement [being] in his library'.[37] The last glimpse we have of John is in his Will, made eleven months before his death. Having set his earthly house in order 'according to the exigency of the present time' and obviously very frail, being barely able to sign his name, yet John proceeds to declare with great assurance of faith,

> I do through the grace of God, in the comfort of a good conscience, humbly commend my soul and spirit into the hands of our Lord Jesus Christ my most gracious and blessed Redeemer, whom I have served, whom I have loved, in whom alone I trust for acceptance with his Father and my Father, in whom also I rejoice in hope to be raised incorruptible in the great day of his appearing, to him be given glory and dominion in the

---

[37] Nichols, *History of Leicestershire*, IV.I:271.

unity of the Father and blessed Spirit,
forever, Amen.

And then, in an echo of Psalm 62, 'My soul waits for thy
salvation O Lord'.[38]

John died on 27 May 1698 aged ninety-four, and was
buried in the chancel of Burbage church three days later,
next to his second wife, Priscilla. The gravestone is no
longer visible, but his epitaph has been recorded: it read
'resting in hope', a reference from Psalm 16:9, 'my flesh
also shall rest in hope'.[39] Many years earlier, John had
explained what that hope of resurrection meant:

> [God's] powerful word, O believing soul,
> shall gather thy scattered dust, and join
> thy crumbled bones; shall burst the
> bands of death and the shackles of the
> grave; the sound of the last trumpet shall
> awake thee from so long a sleep; and
> when that joyful morning shall begin to
> dawn, thou shall have such a summons

---

[38] Will of John St Nicholas, ROLLR, PR/1/103, 47/1698.

[39] Nichols, *History of Leicestershire*, IV.II:464, describes the gravestones of John and Priscilla as being 'on flat stones within the rails of the altar', with the inscriptions reading, 1. 'The noble and virtuous Lady Priscilla Grey, youngest daughter of the right honourable Anthony Grey earl of Kent; a singular pattern of piety and virtue in her single and married state, deceased Sept. 16, 1665, in the 51st year of her age; and lyeth here interred, resting in hope', and 2. 'Here lieth the body of John St Nicholas, esq. husband of the Lady Priscilla, who departed this life May 27, 1698, in the 95th year of his age, resting in hope'.

that thy heart shall leap to hear, and the
prisoner of hope shall come forth.[40]

---

[40] Newberry Library, N MS fol. 68r, Case MS C 991.767.

Select Bibliography

Manuscript Sources

Newberry Library, Chicago, Manuscript Notebook (N MS: Case MS C 991.767).

The Record Office for Leicestershire, Leicester and Rutland: Will of John St Nicholas, PR/1/103, 47/1698. Inventory of John St Nicholas, 48/1698.

Primary Printed Sources

Calamy, Edmund. *An Account of the Ministers, Lecturers, Masters and Fellows of Colleges and Schoolmasters, who were Ejected or Silenced after the Restoration in 1660*, vol. II, 1713.

Davies, H. Neville, ed. *At Vacant Hours: Poems by Thomas St Nicholas and his Family*. Birmingham: University of Birmingham, 2002.

'Guibon Goddard's Journal: July 1653', Pages i–iv in *Diary of Thomas Burton Esq: July 1653–April 1657*. Edited by John Towill Rutt. London, 1828. *British History Online* http://www.british.history.ac.uk/burton-diaries/vol 1/i.iv (accessed 17 August 2022).

Henry, Matthew. *The Lives of Philip and Matthew Henry*. Edited by J. B. Williams. Edinburgh: Banner of Truth, 1974.

Neal, Daniel. *Sermons upon Several Occasions; By the Reverend Mr Matthew Clarke ... to which are added Some Memoirs of his Life, and the Sermon preach'd at his Funeral.* 1727.

Nichols, John. *The History and Antiquities of Leicestershire*, vol. IV, part I, 1807 and part II, 1811.

Palmer, Samuel. *The Nonconformist's Memorial.* 1775.

St Nicholas, John, *The History of Baptism.* London, 1678.

St Nicholas, John, *The Widow's Mite.* London, 1695.

Secondary Sources

Appleby, David J. *Black Bartholomew's Day: Preaching, Polemic and Restoration Nonconformity.* Manchester: Manchester University Press, 2007.

Coffey, John. 'Introduction' in, *The Oxford History of Protestant Dissenting Traditions*, vol. 1. Oxford: Oxford University Press, 2020.

Davies, H. Neville. *St Nicholas, Thomas*, ODNB entry, https://doi.org/10.1093/ref:odnb/66680 (accessed 9 August 2022).

Packer, J. I. 'The Doctrine of Justification Among the Puritans', in *Puritan Papers Vol. 5: 1968–69*. Phillipsburg, NJ: P&R Publishing, 2005.

Woolrych, Austin. *Commonwealth to Protectorate.* Oxford: Oxford University Press, 1982.

Previous St. Antholin Lectures

Lectures from 1991–2000 are compiled in *Pilgrims, Warriors, and Servants: Puritan Wisdom for Today's Church*. Edited by Lee Gatiss.

2001–2010

Peter Adam	Word and Spirit: The Puritan-Quaker Debate
Wallace Benn	Usher on Bishops: A Reforming Ecclesiology
Peter Ackroyd	Strangers to Correction: Christian Discipline and the English Reformation
David Field	"Decalogue" Dod and his Seventeenth Century Bestsellers: A 400th Anniversary Appreciation
Chad B Van Dixhoorn	A Puritan Theology of Preaching
Peter Adam	'To Bring Men to Heaven by Preaching': John Donne's Evangelistic Sermons
Tony Baker	1807–2007 John Newton and the Twenty-First Century
Lee Gatiss	From Life's First Cry: John Owen on Infant Baptism and Infant Salvation
Andrew Atherstone	Evangelical Mission and Anglican Church Order: Charles Simeon Reconsidered
David Holloway	Re-establishing the Christian Faith – and the Public Theology Deficit

Lectures from 2001–2010 are compiled in *Preachers, Pastors, and Ambassadors: Puritan Wisdom for Today's Church*. Edited by Lee Gatiss.

2011–2020

In this series:

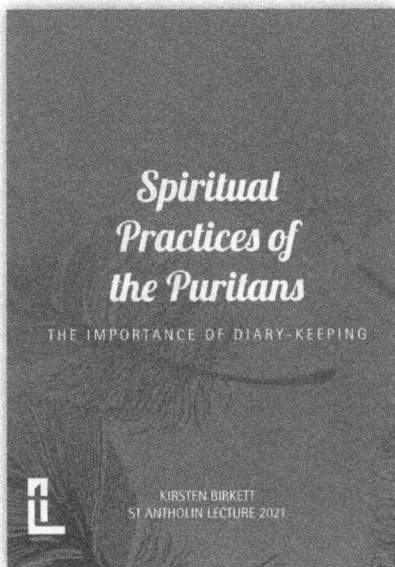

The Puritans wished to live godly lives in heart and thought as well as action. One of the tools they utilised in training their hearts and minds was the practice of diary-writing. In this short overview we see the theory of Puritan diary-writing as worked out by John Beadle, and the inspiring example of the sixteenth-century Puritan Richard Rogers writing about his life.

In our Christian Leadership series:

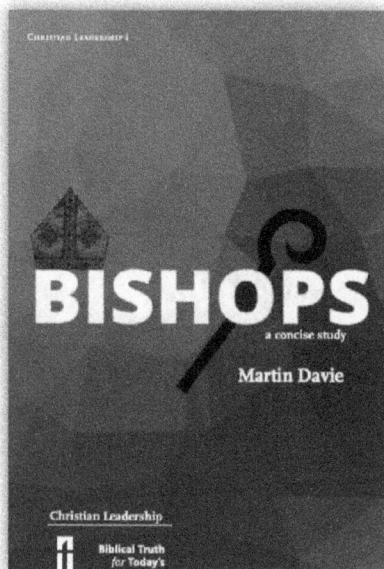

Bishops: A Concise Study summarises the key points of the argument of Martin's major study *Bishops Past, Present and Future* (Gilead Books 2022). It is designed to meet the needs of those who would like to know about the role and importance of bishops in the Church of England, but who would baulk at tackling the 800+ pages of the original book.

This concise study is published in the hope that it will help many in the Church of England, both ordained and lay, to think in a more informed fashion about how bishops should respond to the challenges facing the Church of England at this critical point in its history as it considers how to move forward following the publication of the Living in Love and Faith material.

Also published by the Latimer Trust

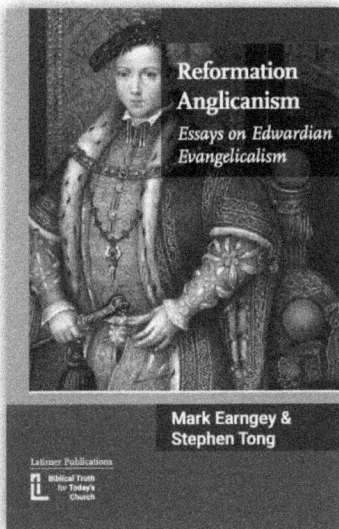

Reformation Anglicanism: Essays on Edwardian Evangelicalism is a superb set of essays arising from the Moore Theological College symposium on Reformation Anglicanism held in 2019. Featuring essays from various reformation scholars, this collection of articles focuses on some foundational documents (e.g. *Book of Homilies, Articles of Religion*) and foundational reformers (e.g. Thomas Cranmer, Martin Bucer, Heinrich Bullinger) involved with the English Reformation, and its Edwardian phase in particular. This edited volume not only offers a sustained focus on the often-neglected mid-Tudor phase of the Reformation but explores new avenues of research on overlooked subjects such as the *45 Articles of Religion*, John Ponet's *Short Catechism*, the *Reformatio Legum Ecclesiasticarum*, the ministry of John Hooper, and the memory of Martin Bucer. Students and scholars alike will benefit from this fresh examination of these anchors of Anglicanism which were hotly contested both then, and now.

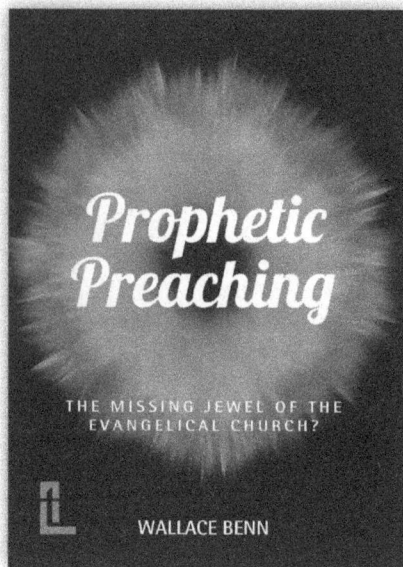

Prophetic Preaching

THE MISSING JEWEL OF THE EVANGELICAL CHURCH?

WALLACE BENN

What is the relationship between prophecy and preaching? Why is preaching not as well thought of as it should be, not as good as it could be, seeing it is the central ingredient in the life if a healthy church? What can we learn from a careful look at Peter's preaching in Acts 2? Writing with over 50 years of ministry experience, Wallace Benn answers these questions and brings a significant challenge to the contemporary church to be the prophetic people God has called us to be.

www.ingramcontent.com/pod-product-compliance
Lightning Source LLC
Chambersburg PA
CBHW020442030426
42337CB00014B/1350